To Yemisi

new Baby

From The Osman family.

## MEDITATIONS FOR NEW MOTHERS

Patricia H. Sprinkle

ZondervanPublishingHouse
*Grand Rapids, Michigan*
*A Division of* HarperCollins*Publishers*

*Dedicated to*

BARNABAS AND DAVID

*—who daily grow in the image of God*

A Gift from God
Copyright © 1988, 1994 by Patricia H. Sprinkle

Requests for information should be addressed to:
Zondervan Publishing House
Grand Rapids, Michigan  49530

ISBN 0-310-41080-0

Interior design by Jamison•Bell Advertising and Design
Cover and interior illustrations by Mitchell Heinz
Cover design by Sharon Wright
Cover calligraphy by Timothy Botts

Printed in the United States of America

94 95 96 97 98 /DC/ 10 9 8 7 6 5 4 3 2 1

This edition is printed on acid-free paper and meets the American National Standards Institute Z39.48 standard.

# Introduction

When I had my first baby, I looked forward to teaching my child about God. I never imagined that in their first year, babies teach us far more about God than we teach them!

I did not realize that when God creates a person in his image, he does so from the very beginning. We who yearn to know God better can learn much about him from those he has recently stamped with his likeness.

Even before my babies were born, I found that my thoughts of the baby were often linked with my thoughts of God. During the year after each birth, I discovered that God used my baby to teach me not only about my role as a parent, but about my role as a child of God, and a member of God's whole family.

My prayer for each one who reads this book is that you and *your* baby will also share in the special joys that come as you teach each other about what it means to be members of God's family.

*Patricia H. Sprinkle*

I wish you'd come, Little One. As I move ponderously about the house or wedge myself between supermarket displays, I am heavy with longing for you to be born. I am eager to see you, hold you, discover just exactly who and what you are. Are you a girl or a boy? Do you have your daddy's hair, or my nose? Hurry, Baby! When you get here, you'll have a lot more room for kicks and stretches than you do now. We'll cuddle and play, have such fun together.

But you are content to slumber where you are. Are you afraid to risk a new environment? Come on, Baby! It's not much of a risk. After all, I'll be here.

And as I wait, impatient with longing, I wonder: Is this how God feels, waiting for us to find him or for us to come back to him when we have drifted away? Does God, too, yearn to stir my spirit as I struggle with my doubts and fears until I take that one final step of faith and say, "Hello. Here I am. I believe!"? How can God stand the waiting?

**Before
I formed you
in the womb
I knew you.**

JEREMIAH 1:5

## My Thoughts, Feelings, and Prayers for My Baby

. . . . . . . . . . . . . . . . . . . . . . . . . . . . . . . . . . . . . . . . . . . . . . . . . . . . . . . . . . . . .
_____
. . . . . . . . . . . . . . . . . . . . . . . . . . . . . . . . . . . . . . . . . . . . . . . . . . . . . . . . . . . . .
_____
. . . . . . . . . . . . . . . . . . . . . . . . . . . . . . . . . . . . . . . . . . . . . . . . . . . . . . . . . . . . .
_____
. . . . . . . . . . . . . . . . . . . . . . . . . . . . . . . . . . . . . . . . . . . . . . . . . . . . . . . . . . . . .
_____
. . . . . . . . . . . . . . . . . . . . . . . . . . . . . . . . . . . . . . . . . . . . . . . . . . . . . . . . . . . . .
_____
. . . . . . . . . . . . . . . . . . . . . . . . . . . . . . . . . . . . . . . . . . . . . . . . . . . . . . . . . . . . .
_____
. . . . . . . . . . . . . . . . . . . . . . . . . . . . . . . . . . . . . . . . . . . . . . . . . . . . . . . . . . . . .
_____
. . . . . . . . . . . . . . . . . . . . . . . . . . . . . . . . . . . . . . . . . . . . . . . . . . . . . . . . . . . . .
_____
. . . . . . . . . . . . . . . . . . . . . . . . . . . . . . . . . . . . . . . . . . . . . . . . . . . . . . . . . . . . .
_____
. . . . . . . . . . . . . . . . . . . . . . . . . . . . . . . . . . . . . . . . . . . . . . . . . . . . . . . . . . . . .
_____
. . . . . . . . . . . . . . . . . . . . . . . . . . . . . . . . . . . . . . . . . . . . . . . . . . . . . . . . . . . . .
_____
. . . . . . . . . . . . . . . . . . . . . . . . . . . . . . . . . . . . . . . . . . . . . . . . . . . . . . . . . . . . .
_____
. . . . . . . . . . . . . . . . . . . . . . . . . . . . . . . . . . . . . . . . . . . . . . . . . . . . . . . . . . . . .
_____
. . . . . . . . . . . . . . . . . . . . . . . . . . . . . . . . . . . . . . . . . . . . . . . . . . . . . . . . . . . . .
_____
. . . . . . . . . . . . . . . . . . . . . . . . . . . . . . . . . . . . . . . . . . . . . . . . . . . . . . . . . . . . .
_____
. . . . . . . . . . . . . . . . . . . . . . . . . . . . . . . . . . . . . . . . . . . . . . . . . . . . . . . . . . . . .
_____
. . . . . . . . . . . . . . . . . . . . . . . . . . . . . . . . . . . . . . . . . . . . . . . . . . . . . . . . . . . . .
_____
. . . . . . . . . . . . . . . . . . . . . . . . . . . . . . . . . . . . . . . . . . . . . . . . . . . . . . . . . . . . .
_____

**W**elcome to our family, Beloved One!

Most of today I spent holding you, curled into a ball on my chest. I cradled your grapefruit head against my chin. Now you lie on your tummy in your bassinet beside my bed. As you lift your tiny rear, give a lurch, and slide one knee across the sheet, I gasp in comprehension. *That's* what you were doing these past few days!

As I gently stroke your back, I marvel. Yesterday you were only a word: *Baby*. Only a ripple within me, a dream, a hope. Now today you are YOU: someone with a name, a face, a personality of your very own. Yesterday you were someone I could talk about. Today you are someone I can talk *to*. A Bible phrase comes to my mind: "the Word became flesh."

By being born, you help me understand your former mystery, your reality. Isn't that what Jesus did? He made the nebulous word *God* into a person—someone with a name, a personality. You become very holy to me, Child, when I realize that when God wanted to show exactly what he was like, he sent a baby.

> **I**n the beginning was the Word. . . . The Word became flesh and made his dwelling among us.
>
> JOHN 1:1, 14

## My Thoughts, Feelings, and Prayers for My Baby

. . . . . . . . . . . . . . . . . . . . . . . . . . . . . . . . . . . . . . . . . . . . . . . . . . . . . . .
. . . . . . . . . . . . . . . . . . . . . . . . . . . . . . . . . . . . . . . . . . . . . . . . . . . . . . .
. . . . . . . . . . . . . . . . . . . . . . . . . . . . . . . . . . . . . . . . . . . . . . . . . . . . . . .
. . . . . . . . . . . . . . . . . . . . . . . . . . . . . . . . . . . . . . . . . . . . . . . . . . . . . . .
. . . . . . . . . . . . . . . . . . . . . . . . . . . . . . . . . . . . . . . . . . . . . . . . . . . . . . .
. . . . . . . . . . . . . . . . . . . . . . . . . . . . . . . . . . . . . . . . . . . . . . . . . . . . . . .
. . . . . . . . . . . . . . . . . . . . . . . . . . . . . . . . . . . . . . . . . . . . . . . . . . . . . . .
. . . . . . . . . . . . . . . . . . . . . . . . . . . . . . . . . . . . . . . . . . . . . . . . . . . . . . .
. . . . . . . . . . . . . . . . . . . . . . . . . . . . . . . . . . . . . . . . . . . . . . . . . . . . . . .
. . . . . . . . . . . . . . . . . . . . . . . . . . . . . . . . . . . . . . . . . . . . . . . . . . . . . . .
. . . . . . . . . . . . . . . . . . . . . . . . . . . . . . . . . . . . . . . . . . . . . . . . . . . . . . .
. . . . . . . . . . . . . . . . . . . . . . . . . . . . . . . . . . . . . . . . . . . . . . . . . . . . . . .
. . . . . . . . . . . . . . . . . . . . . . . . . . . . . . . . . . . . . . . . . . . . . . . . . . . . . . .
. . . . . . . . . . . . . . . . . . . . . . . . . . . . . . . . . . . . . . . . . . . . . . . . . . . . . . .
. . . . . . . . . . . . . . . . . . . . . . . . . . . . . . . . . . . . . . . . . . . . . . . . . . . . . . .
. . . . . . . . . . . . . . . . . . . . . . . . . . . . . . . . . . . . . . . . . . . . . . . . . . . . . . .
. . . . . . . . . . . . . . . . . . . . . . . . . . . . . . . . . . . . . . . . . . . . . . . . . . . . . . .
. . . . . . . . . . . . . . . . . . . . . . . . . . . . . . . . . . . . . . . . . . . . . . . . . . . . . . .
. . . . . . . . . . . . . . . . . . . . . . . . . . . . . . . . . . . . . . . . . . . . . . . . . . . . . . .
. . . . . . . . . . . . . . . . . . . . . . . . . . . . . . . . . . . . . . . . . . . . . . . . . . . . . . .

## One Day Old

**B**efore you came, I knew that I would love you. I knew that there was room in my heart for you. But I thought that it would take time for us to bond; that my love for you would grow a little each day. After all, that's how love is supposed to happen.

What a surprise! They brought you to me for the very first time. As I held you and looked into the haze of your newborn eyes, I knew that I had been wrong. My love for you is complete. So overwhelming that I'm afraid to let you go — even to the arms of Nurse.

I grow anxious at the thought of losing you. My imagination works overtime. Will I drift off to sleep and let you fall? Are you really breathing?

God alone knows how far we will travel together on earth, Little One. Today I am aware of how fragile you are, and I cherish every hour, every minute we have together.

## My Thoughts, Feelings, and Prayers for My Baby

. . . . . . . . . . . . . . . . . . . . . . . . . . . . . . . . . . . . . . . . . . . . . . . . . . . . . . . . . . . . . . . . . . . . . . . . . . . . .

. . . . . . . . . . . . . . . . . . . . . . . . . . . . . . . . . . . . . . . . . . . . . . . . . . . . . . . . . . . . . . . . . . . . . . . . . . . . .

. . . . . . . . . . . . . . . . . . . . . . . . . . . . . . . . . . . . . . . . . . . . . . . . . . . . . . . . . . . . . . . . . . . . . . . . . . . . .

. . . . . . . . . . . . . . . . . . . . . . . . . . . . . . . . . . . . . . . . . . . . . . . . . . . . . . . . . . . . . . . . . . . . . . . . . . . . .

. . . . . . . . . . . . . . . . . . . . . . . . . . . . . . . . . . . . . . . . . . . . . . . . . . . . . . . . . . . . . . . . . . . . . . . . . . . . .

. . . . . . . . . . . . . . . . . . . . . . . . . . . . . . . . . . . . . . . . . . . . . . . . . . . . . . . . . . . . . . . . . . . . . . . . . . . . .

. . . . . . . . . . . . . . . . . . . . . . . . . . . . . . . . . . . . . . . . . . . . . . . . . . . . . . . . . . . . . . . . . . . . . . . . . . . . .

. . . . . . . . . . . . . . . . . . . . . . . . . . . . . . . . . . . . . . . . . . . . . . . . . . . . . . . . . . . . . . . . . . . . . . . . . . . . .

. . . . . . . . . . . . . . . . . . . . . . . . . . . . . . . . . . . . . . . . . . . . . . . . . . . . . . . . . . . . . . . . . . . . . . . . . . . . .

. . . . . . . . . . . . . . . . . . . . . . . . . . . . . . . . . . . . . . . . . . . . . . . . . . . . . . . . . . . . . . . . . . . . . . . . . . . . .

. . . . . . . . . . . . . . . . . . . . . . . . . . . . . . . . . . . . . . . . . . . . . . . . . . . . . . . . . . . . . . . . . . . . . . . . . . . . .

. . . . . . . . . . . . . . . . . . . . . . . . . . . . . . . . . . . . . . . . . . . . . . . . . . . . . . . . . . . . . . . . . . . . . . . . . . . . .

. . . . . . . . . . . . . . . . . . . . . . . . . . . . . . . . . . . . . . . . . . . . . . . . . . . . . . . . . . . . . . . . . . . . . . . . . . . . .

. . . . . . . . . . . . . . . . . . . . . . . . . . . . . . . . . . . . . . . . . . . . . . . . . . . . . . . . . . . . . . . . . . . . . . . . . . . . .

. . . . . . . . . . . . . . . . . . . . . . . . . . . . . . . . . . . . . . . . . . . . . . . . . . . . . . . . . . . . . . . . . . . . . . . . . . . . .

. . . . . . . . . . . . . . . . . . . . . . . . . . . . . . . . . . . . . . . . . . . . . . . . . . . . . . . . . . . . . . . . . . . . . . . . . . . . .

. . . . . . . . . . . . . . . . . . . . . . . . . . . . . . . . . . . . . . . . . . . . . . . . . . . . . . . . . . . . . . . . . . . . . . . . . . . . .

. . . . . . . . . . . . . . . . . . . . . . . . . . . . . . . . . . . . . . . . . . . . . . . . . . . . . . . . . . . . . . . . . . . . . . . . . . . . .

. . . . . . . . . . . . . . . . . . . . . . . . . . . . . . . . . . . . . . . . . . . . . . . . . . . . . . . . . . . . . . . . . . . . . . . . . . . . .

. . . . . . . . . . . . . . . . . . . . . . . . . . . . . . . . . . . . . . . . . . . . . . . . . . . . . . . . . . . . . . . . . . . . . . . . . . . . .

. . . . . . . . . . . . . . . . . . . . . . . . . . . . . . . . . . . . . . . . . . . . . . . . . . . . . . . . . . . . . . . . . . . . . . . . . . . . .

# Three Days Old

**W**ell, Little One, it is time to go home.

I assemble your clothes and begin to change you from your hospital shirt and diaper into new ones. These are your very own, Child—the others were merely borrowed. But those borrowed ones are the only ones you've ever known, and so, as I try to dress you, you protest mightily. When I move about the room packing up, you screw up your face and cry lustily. Don't you want to go home?

We've prepared a very special place for you—a crib of your own, a chest full of clothes, a basket of toys and books. There are warm blankets there, and a colorful mobile to swing above your crib.

I know this room is all you've known, that you've been here your whole lifetime. I understand that it is hard to leave. But trust me, Little One. There is a big, beautiful world out there.

Jesus said, "I go to prepare a place for you." Jesus was talking about dying. But he could have been talking about change—any change. Maybe he was saying to me what I'm saying to you. "Cheer up, Child. I've already been there, getting things ready. Come with me to a big, new life!"

> **In my Father's house are many rooms; . . . I am going there to prepare a place for you.**
>
> JOHN 14:2

## My Thoughts, Feelings, and Prayers for My Baby

.............................................................................
.............................................................................
.............................................................................
.............................................................................
.............................................................................
.............................................................................
.............................................................................
.............................................................................
.............................................................................
.............................................................................
.............................................................................
.............................................................................
.............................................................................
.............................................................................
.............................................................................
.............................................................................
.............................................................................
.............................................................................
.............................................................................
.............................................................................
.............................................................................
.............................................................................
.............................................................................

# One Week Old

Lying very close to you, my chin nestled on your fuzzy crown, I almost wonder if you're still alive, Little One. You are so deep in sleep that you do not move.

But then I feel your warm breath on my throat. Each puff reassures me that you are strong, vital, alive.

Isn't it interesting that the Hebrew word for spirit— *ruach* —also means breath? The breath of God moved across the waters in Creation. The breath of God blew like a whirlwind at Pentecost. The breath of God comes into our lives and stirs us with power and love.

Each puff of the Holy Spirit reassures us that God is strong, vital, alive!

## My Thoughts, Feelings, and Prayers for My Baby

# Ten Days Old

Who could have imagined that a tiny baby could take up so much time? For three days I have planned to get to the store for potting soil and pots to transplant the geraniums. But day after day, I find that I hardly have time for a shower—all my time is full of you.

I pick up the laundry, then lay it down to change you. I gather dirty dishes, then lay them down to feed you. I pick up my car keys, but lay them down because you've already started your nap. Jesus said we are to lay down our lives for other people. Is this what he meant? Does laying down my life mean laying down the laundry, the dishes, the novel I'd saved to read until after you were born?

Society tells me to do my own thing, to meet my own needs. These are worthwhile goals, but Jesus points me to a greater good. A love that recognizes my own needs and deliberately, joyfully puts them aside for someone else. It looks like you, Little One, have come to help me learn that kind of love!

> **G**reater love has
> no one than this,
> that he lay down his life
> for his friends.
>
> JOHN 15:13

## My Thoughts, Feelings, and Prayers for My Baby

........................................................................

........................................................................

........................................................................

........................................................................

........................................................................

........................................................................

........................................................................

........................................................................

........................................................................

........................................................................

........................................................................

........................................................................

........................................................................

........................................................................

........................................................................

........................................................................

........................................................................

........................................................................

........................................................................

........................................................................

*T*'m coming, Child.

I was sitting in my room having a time of prayer when I heard your first little whimper, and I knew you were hungry. Since that first cry, I've been getting ready to feed you, assuring you softly that you are going to eat soon. But still you cry louder and louder. As we settle into our rocker, you are screaming with rage.

Hush, Little One. Do you really think I will refuse you what you need? Don't you know yet how much I love you?

Now, while you nurse, I will get back to the prayer I left when you began to cry. Where was I? Oh, yes. I was reminding God again that I need...

What's that? I thought I heard Someone whisper, "I heard you the first time, too. Don't you know how much I love YOU?"

> **A**sk and
> it will be
> given to you.
>
> MATTHEW 7:7

## My Thoughts, Feelings, and Prayers for My Baby

. . . . . . . . . . . . . . . . . . . . . . . . . . . . . . . . . . . . . . . . . . . . . . . . . . . . . . . . . . . . . . .

. . . . . . . . . . . . . . . . . . . . . . . . . . . . . . . . . . . . . . . . . . . . . . . . . . . . . . . . . . . . . . .

. . . . . . . . . . . . . . . . . . . . . . . . . . . . . . . . . . . . . . . . . . . . . . . . . . . . . . . . . . . . . . .

. . . . . . . . . . . . . . . . . . . . . . . . . . . . . . . . . . . . . . . . . . . . . . . . . . . . . . . . . . . . . . .

. . . . . . . . . . . . . . . . . . . . . . . . . . . . . . . . . . . . . . . . . . . . . . . . . . . . . . . . . . . . . . .

. . . . . . . . . . . . . . . . . . . . . . . . . . . . . . . . . . . . . . . . . . . . . . . . . . . . . . . . . . . . . . .

. . . . . . . . . . . . . . . . . . . . . . . . . . . . . . . . . . . . . . . . . . . . . . . . . . . . . . . . . . . . . . .

. . . . . . . . . . . . . . . . . . . . . . . . . . . . . . . . . . . . . . . . . . . . . . . . . . . . . . . . . . . . . . .

. . . . . . . . . . . . . . . . . . . . . . . . . . . . . . . . . . . . . . . . . . . . . . . . . . . . . . . . . . . . . . .

. . . . . . . . . . . . . . . . . . . . . . . . . . . . . . . . . . . . . . . . . . . . . . . . . . . . . . . . . . . . . . .

. . . . . . . . . . . . . . . . . . . . . . . . . . . . . . . . . . . . . . . . . . . . . . . . . . . . . . . . . . . . . . .

. . . . . . . . . . . . . . . . . . . . . . . . . . . . . . . . . . . . . . . . . . . . . . . . . . . . . . . . . . . . . . .

. . . . . . . . . . . . . . . . . . . . . . . . . . . . . . . . . . . . . . . . . . . . . . . . . . . . . . . . . . . . . . .

. . . . . . . . . . . . . . . . . . . . . . . . . . . . . . . . . . . . . . . . . . . . . . . . . . . . . . . . . . . . . . .

. . . . . . . . . . . . . . . . . . . . . . . . . . . . . . . . . . . . . . . . . . . . . . . . . . . . . . . . . . . . . . .

. . . . . . . . . . . . . . . . . . . . . . . . . . . . . . . . . . . . . . . . . . . . . . . . . . . . . . . . . . . . . . .

. . . . . . . . . . . . . . . . . . . . . . . . . . . . . . . . . . . . . . . . . . . . . . . . . . . . . . . . . . . . . . .

. . . . . . . . . . . . . . . . . . . . . . . . . . . . . . . . . . . . . . . . . . . . . . . . . . . . . . . . . . . . . . .

. . . . . . . . . . . . . . . . . . . . . . . . . . . . . . . . . . . . . . . . . . . . . . . . . . . . . . . . . . . . . . .

. . . . . . . . . . . . . . . . . . . . . . . . . . . . . . . . . . . . . . . . . . . . . . . . . . . . . . . . . . . . . . .

. . . . . . . . . . . . . . . . . . . . . . . . . . . . . . . . . . . . . . . . . . . . . . . . . . . . . . . . . . . . . . .

# Seventeen Days Old

**S**ometimes, some very special times, as I sit rocking you in the dimness, time seems to part gently like a dimple on a pool's surface. Together we sink into a marvelous gift of timelessness.

The Greeks have a word for it: *kairos*. That means "the strategic time," or "God's time." A time that is not defined by a clock.

As your tiny head melts into the curve of my arm and our bodies fuse in warmth, I lose all sense of time passing by.

It is not that time stands still, but rather that we no longer stand within time. We become a part of time itself.

Thank you, Small One, for leading me to the threshold of eternity.

> **I am the Alpha and the Omega, the First and the Last, the Beginning and the End.**
>
> REVELATION 22:13

## My Thoughts, Feelings, and Prayers for My Baby

. . . . . . . . . . . . . . . . . . . . . . . . . . . . . . . . . . . . . . . . . . . . . . . . . . . . . . . . . . . . . . . . . . . . . . . . . . . . . . . . . . . . . . . .

. . . . . . . . . . . . . . . . . . . . . . . . . . . . . . . . . . . . . . . . . . . . . . . . . . . . . . . . . . . . . . . . . . . . . . . . . . . . . . . . . . . . . . . .

. . . . . . . . . . . . . . . . . . . . . . . . . . . . . . . . . . . . . . . . . . . . . . . . . . . . . . . . . . . . . . . . . . . . . . . . . . . . . . . . . . . . . . . .

. . . . . . . . . . . . . . . . . . . . . . . . . . . . . . . . . . . . . . . . . . . . . . . . . . . . . . . . . . . . . . . . . . . . . . . . . . . . . . . . . . . . . . . .

. . . . . . . . . . . . . . . . . . . . . . . . . . . . . . . . . . . . . . . . . . . . . . . . . . . . . . . . . . . . . . . . . . . . . . . . . . . . . . . . . . . . . . . .

. . . . . . . . . . . . . . . . . . . . . . . . . . . . . . . . . . . . . . . . . . . . . . . . . . . . . . . . . . . . . . . . . . . . . . . . . . . . . . . . . . . . . . . .

. . . . . . . . . . . . . . . . . . . . . . . . . . . . . . . . . . . . . . . . . . . . . . . . . . . . . . . . . . . . . . . . . . . . . . . . . . . . . . . . . . . . . . . .

. . . . . . . . . . . . . . . . . . . . . . . . . . . . . . . . . . . . . . . . . . . . . . . . . . . . . . . . . . . . . . . . . . . . . . . . . . . . . . . . . . . . . . . .

. . . . . . . . . . . . . . . . . . . . . . . . . . . . . . . . . . . . . . . . . . . . . . . . . . . . . . . . . . . . . . . . . . . . . . . . . . . . . . . . . . . . . . . .

. . . . . . . . . . . . . . . . . . . . . . . . . . . . . . . . . . . . . . . . . . . . . . . . . . . . . . . . . . . . . . . . . . . . . . . . . . . . . . . . . . . . . . . .

. . . . . . . . . . . . . . . . . . . . . . . . . . . . . . . . . . . . . . . . . . . . . . . . . . . . . . . . . . . . . . . . . . . . . . . . . . . . . . . . . . . . . . . .

. . . . . . . . . . . . . . . . . . . . . . . . . . . . . . . . . . . . . . . . . . . . . . . . . . . . . . . . . . . . . . . . . . . . . . . . . . . . . . . . . . . . . . . .

. . . . . . . . . . . . . . . . . . . . . . . . . . . . . . . . . . . . . . . . . . . . . . . . . . . . . . . . . . . . . . . . . . . . . . . . . . . . . . . . . . . . . . . .

. . . . . . . . . . . . . . . . . . . . . . . . . . . . . . . . . . . . . . . . . . . . . . . . . . . . . . . . . . . . . . . . . . . . . . . . . . . . . . . . . . . . . . . .

. . . . . . . . . . . . . . . . . . . . . . . . . . . . . . . . . . . . . . . . . . . . . . . . . . . . . . . . . . . . . . . . . . . . . . . . . . . . . . . . . . . . . . . .

. . . . . . . . . . . . . . . . . . . . . . . . . . . . . . . . . . . . . . . . . . . . . . . . . . . . . . . . . . . . . . . . . . . . . . . . . . . . . . . . . . . . . . . .

. . . . . . . . . . . . . . . . . . . . . . . . . . . . . . . . . . . . . . . . . . . . . . . . . . . . . . . . . . . . . . . . . . . . . . . . . . . . . . . . . . . . . . . .

. . . . . . . . . . . . . . . . . . . . . . . . . . . . . . . . . . . . . . . . . . . . . . . . . . . . . . . . . . . . . . . . . . . . . . . . . . . . . . . . . . . . . . . .

. . . . . . . . . . . . . . . . . . . . . . . . . . . . . . . . . . . . . . . . . . . . . . . . . . . . . . . . . . . . . . . . . . . . . . . . . . . . . . . . . . . . . . . .

. . . . . . . . . . . . . . . . . . . . . . . . . . . . . . . . . . . . . . . . . . . . . . . . . . . . . . . . . . . . . . . . . . . . . . . . . . . . . . . . . . . . . . . .

. . . . . . . . . . . . . . . . . . . . . . . . . . . . . . . . . . . . . . . . . . . . . . . . . . . . . . . . . . . . . . . . . . . . . . . . . . . . . . . . . . . . . . . .

**W**hat do you see, Little One, as your eyes focus far beyond my shoulder while I bend over your crib? What do you hear? What do you think about, so intent on something I cannot see?

Today, for the first time, I realize that you and I are separate, and the thought makes me a little afraid. I know, of course, that you have been a separate person for a long time, even when you were cradled within me, but I have grown so accustomed to thinking of you as a part of me. Today I realize that one day you will grow up—and away.

As you grow, you will see, hear, and believe things that are not what I see, hear, or believe. You may like things that I dislike, and dislike some things that I love. God and you together may even choose for you a purpose, a path, that is not at all what I would have chosen for you.

Don't hurry, Child. I know that it will not be easy to let you go. I need time to pray that God will give me grace not only to bear, but also to encourage your growth toward independence. I will pray too, Little One, that whatever path you take, you will walk with God.

> **I urge you to live a life worthy of the calling you have received.**
>
> EPHESIANS 4:1

## My Thoughts, Feelings, and Prayers for My Baby

e both learned an important lesson today, Little One.

It was a busy day, with lots of company and a hectic schedule. My "superwoman" complex kept me rushing here and there, and when you got hungry I fed you almost without thinking, continuing my conversations and expecting you to hurry to meet my schedule.

But you weren't willing to hurry. You whined and fretted, growing tense and anxious.

Then a wise friend suggested we go off into a quiet room, just you and me. We rocked and shared a smile. (You did smile, didn't you?) And in peace, you nursed contentedly.

Once again God was teaching me through you. Like you, God doesn't want to be squeezed into the corners of my busy-ness. Like you, I get my best feedings in quiet, private moments of total communion.

Why do I expose you to hectic feedings and myself to hectic prayers when I know the best nourishment is available in quiet corners?

**Be still, and know that I am God.**

PSALM 46:10

## My Thoughts, Feelings, and Prayers for My Baby

. . . . . . . . . . . . . . . . . . . . . . . . . . . . . . . . . . . . . . . . . . . . . . . . . . . . . . . . . . . . . . . . . . . . . . . . . . . . . . . . . . . . . . . . . . .

. . . . . . . . . . . . . . . . . . . . . . . . . . . . . . . . . . . . . . . . . . . . . . . . . . . . . . . . . . . . . . . . . . . . . . . . . . . . . . . . . . . . . . . . . . .

. . . . . . . . . . . . . . . . . . . . . . . . . . . . . . . . . . . . . . . . . . . . . . . . . . . . . . . . . . . . . . . . . . . . . . . . . . . . . . . . . . . . . . . . . . .

. . . . . . . . . . . . . . . . . . . . . . . . . . . . . . . . . . . . . . . . . . . . . . . . . . . . . . . . . . . . . . . . . . . . . . . . . . . . . . . . . . . . . . . . . . .

. . . . . . . . . . . . . . . . . . . . . . . . . . . . . . . . . . . . . . . . . . . . . . . . . . . . . . . . . . . . . . . . . . . . . . . . . . . . . . . . . . . . . . . . . . .

. . . . . . . . . . . . . . . . . . . . . . . . . . . . . . . . . . . . . . . . . . . . . . . . . . . . . . . . . . . . . . . . . . . . . . . . . . . . . . . . . . . . . . . . . . .

. . . . . . . . . . . . . . . . . . . . . . . . . . . . . . . . . . . . . . . . . . . . . . . . . . . . . . . . . . . . . . . . . . . . . . . . . . . . . . . . . . . . . . . . . . .

. . . . . . . . . . . . . . . . . . . . . . . . . . . . . . . . . . . . . . . . . . . . . . . . . . . . . . . . . . . . . . . . . . . . . . . . . . . . . . . . . . . . . . . . . . .

. . . . . . . . . . . . . . . . . . . . . . . . . . . . . . . . . . . . . . . . . . . . . . . . . . . . . . . . . . . . . . . . . . . . . . . . . . . . . . . . . . . . . . . . . . .

. . . . . . . . . . . . . . . . . . . . . . . . . . . . . . . . . . . . . . . . . . . . . . . . . . . . . . . . . . . . . . . . . . . . . . . . . . . . . . . . . . . . . . . . . . .

. . . . . . . . . . . . . . . . . . . . . . . . . . . . . . . . . . . . . . . . . . . . . . . . . . . . . . . . . . . . . . . . . . . . . . . . . . . . . . . . . . . . . . . . . . .

. . . . . . . . . . . . . . . . . . . . . . . . . . . . . . . . . . . . . . . . . . . . . . . . . . . . . . . . . . . . . . . . . . . . . . . . . . . . . . . . . . . . . . . . . . .

. . . . . . . . . . . . . . . . . . . . . . . . . . . . . . . . . . . . . . . . . . . . . . . . . . . . . . . . . . . . . . . . . . . . . . . . . . . . . . . . . . . . . . . . . . .

. . . . . . . . . . . . . . . . . . . . . . . . . . . . . . . . . . . . . . . . . . . . . . . . . . . . . . . . . . . . . . . . . . . . . . . . . . . . . . . . . . . . . . . . . . .

. . . . . . . . . . . . . . . . . . . . . . . . . . . . . . . . . . . . . . . . . . . . . . . . . . . . . . . . . . . . . . . . . . . . . . . . . . . . . . . . . . . . . . . . . . .

. . . . . . . . . . . . . . . . . . . . . . . . . . . . . . . . . . . . . . . . . . . . . . . . . . . . . . . . . . . . . . . . . . . . . . . . . . . . . . . . . . . . . . . . . . .

. . . . . . . . . . . . . . . . . . . . . . . . . . . . . . . . . . . . . . . . . . . . . . . . . . . . . . . . . . . . . . . . . . . . . . . . . . . . . . . . . . . . . . . . . . .

. . . . . . . . . . . . . . . . . . . . . . . . . . . . . . . . . . . . . . . . . . . . . . . . . . . . . . . . . . . . . . . . . . . . . . . . . . . . . . . . . . . . . . . . . . .

. . . . . . . . . . . . . . . . . . . . . . . . . . . . . . . . . . . . . . . . . . . . . . . . . . . . . . . . . . . . . . . . . . . . . . . . . . . . . . . . . . . . . . . . . . .

. . . . . . . . . . . . . . . . . . . . . . . . . . . . . . . . . . . . . . . . . . . . . . . . . . . . . . . . . . . . . . . . . . . . . . . . . . . . . . . . . . . . . . . . . . .

## Five Weeks Old

How special, Beloved. You are beginning to know me! Even in a room full of people, you turn your head toward my voice. How your face lights up when I speak! Soon, the experts tell me, you will even choose my face in a crowd, but for now you go only by the voice. When you get anxious, nobody else will do. Only my voice, or sometimes that of your daddy, can calm you.

Watching you strain to listen makes me want to improve my own listening skills. I want to hear the voice of my heavenly Parent; to pick him out from all the others. Like you, when I need comfort, nobody else will do. Show me by your example how to tune my ears to the one voice my heart yearns to hear.

> **I am the good shepherd; I know my sheep and my sheep know me.**
>
> JOHN 10:14

24

## My Thoughts, Feelings, and Prayers for My Baby

.......................................................................

.......................................................................

.......................................................................

.......................................................................

.......................................................................

.......................................................................

.......................................................................

.......................................................................

.......................................................................

.......................................................................

.......................................................................

.......................................................................

.......................................................................

.......................................................................

.......................................................................

.......................................................................

.......................................................................

.......................................................................

.......................................................................

.......................................................................

.......................................................................

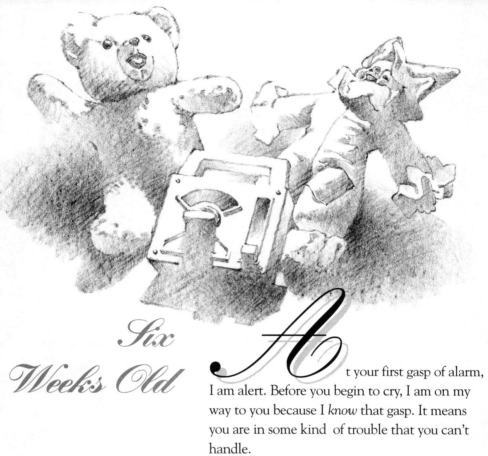

## Six Weeks Old

At your first gasp of alarm, I am alert. Before you begin to cry, I am on my way to you because I *know* that gasp. It means you are in some kind of trouble that you can't handle.

What is it this time? Has your blanket covered your face again? Did the toy you were holding tumble to the floor? Or, has the music box wound down?

Little babies have little troubles, but they are very real. That's why I hurry to your side. I want you to feel that you are protected, watched over.

If I delay, I feel Someone within me, nudging me along. And guess what? As I learn to listen for your sounds of alarm, my ears are being tuned to hear alarm in others. Is God using me to be an ever-present help to those in trouble?

**God is our refuge and strength, an ever-present help in trouble.**

PSALM 46:1

# MY THOUGHTS, FEELINGS, AND PRAYERS FOR MY BABY

...........................................................................

...........................................................................

...........................................................................

...........................................................................

...........................................................................

...........................................................................

...........................................................................

...........................................................................

...........................................................................

...........................................................................

...........................................................................

...........................................................................

...........................................................................

...........................................................................

...........................................................................

...........................................................................

...........................................................................

...........................................................................

...........................................................................

...........................................................................

...........................................................................

## Seven Weeks Old

My child, you are so basic. Your relationship to me consists almost entirely of "give me" (food, a blanket), "take it away" (an uncomfortable diaper), "love me" (hold me) and, sometimes, "I love you, too."

You make me think about my relationship to God. I realize how many of my prayers to him consist only of "give me," "take it away," "love me" and, only sometimes, "I love you, too."

But every day I see that you are learning to give, Child. To hug, to reach out, to coo with delight. I need to learn to give more to God, too. If I am to help you grow up, I need to grow myself.

As we grow together we'll learn to communicate more maturely. But let's not forget that Jesus always began his prayers with the childish *Abba*, "Daddy." God is Daddy to us all.

## My Thoughts, Feelings, and Prayers for My Baby

.....................................................................
.....................................................................
.....................................................................
.....................................................................
.....................................................................
.....................................................................
.....................................................................
.....................................................................
.....................................................................
.....................................................................
.....................................................................
.....................................................................
.....................................................................
.....................................................................
.....................................................................
.....................................................................
.....................................................................
.....................................................................
.....................................................................
.....................................................................
.....................................................................
.....................................................................
.....................................................................

**G**randmother's car just pulled away, taking you with her. It's the first time you have ever gone anywhere without me, Little One, and I found myself watching her car until it was out of sight.

I should have been planning my free afternoon, but instead I could only think about the accidents that could happen, the worries that might be going on behind your puckered little brow. Again I remember how fragile you are, how easily you could break. When we brought you home from the hospital, how slowly I made your daddy drive! And that first night, how often I got up to be sure that you were still breathing! By now I am used to driving around with you and am accustomed to your almost breathless sleep. But when Grandma's car disappeared, I trembled with fear.

I think it is good for me to remember again how fragile you are, Child. It makes me gentler with you. It also reminds me how fragile all people are, even those who look big and strong. Keep reminding me of how easily people break, Little One, until I learn to be gentle with everyone.

**L**et your
gentleness
be evident
to all.

PHILIPPIANS 4:5

My Thoughts, Feelings, and Prayers for My Baby

. . . . . . . . . . . . . . . . . . . . . . . . . . . . . . . . . . . . . . . . . . . . . . . . . . . . . . . . . . . . . . . . . . . . . . . . . . .
. . . . . . . . . . . . . . . . . . . . . . . . . . . . . . . . . . . . . . . . . . . . . . . . . . . . . . . . . . . . . . . . . . . . . . . . . . .
. . . . . . . . . . . . . . . . . . . . . . . . . . . . . . . . . . . . . . . . . . . . . . . . . . . . . . . . . . . . . . . . . . . . . . . . . . .
. . . . . . . . . . . . . . . . . . . . . . . . . . . . . . . . . . . . . . . . . . . . . . . . . . . . . . . . . . . . . . . . . . . . . . . . . . .
. . . . . . . . . . . . . . . . . . . . . . . . . . . . . . . . . . . . . . . . . . . . . . . . . . . . . . . . . . . . . . . . . . . . . . . . . . .
. . . . . . . . . . . . . . . . . . . . . . . . . . . . . . . . . . . . . . . . . . . . . . . . . . . . . . . . . . . . . . . . . . . . . . . . . . .
. . . . . . . . . . . . . . . . . . . . . . . . . . . . . . . . . . . . . . . . . . . . . . . . . . . . . . . . . . . . . . . . . . . . . . . . . . .
. . . . . . . . . . . . . . . . . . . . . . . . . . . . . . . . . . . . . . . . . . . . . . . . . . . . . . . . . . . . . . . . . . . . . . . . . . .
. . . . . . . . . . . . . . . . . . . . . . . . . . . . . . . . . . . . . . . . . . . . . . . . . . . . . . . . . . . . . . . . . . . . . . . . . . .
. . . . . . . . . . . . . . . . . . . . . . . . . . . . . . . . . . . . . . . . . . . . . . . . . . . . . . . . . . . . . . . . . . . . . . . . . . .
. . . . . . . . . . . . . . . . . . . . . . . . . . . . . . . . . . . . . . . . . . . . . . . . . . . . . . . . . . . . . . . . . . . . . . . . . . .
. . . . . . . . . . . . . . . . . . . . . . . . . . . . . . . . . . . . . . . . . . . . . . . . . . . . . . . . . . . . . . . . . . . . . . . . . . .
. . . . . . . . . . . . . . . . . . . . . . . . . . . . . . . . . . . . . . . . . . . . . . . . . . . . . . . . . . . . . . . . . . . . . . . . . . .
. . . . . . . . . . . . . . . . . . . . . . . . . . . . . . . . . . . . . . . . . . . . . . . . . . . . . . . . . . . . . . . . . . . . . . . . . . .
. . . . . . . . . . . . . . . . . . . . . . . . . . . . . . . . . . . . . . . . . . . . . . . . . . . . . . . . . . . . . . . . . . . . . . . . . . .
. . . . . . . . . . . . . . . . . . . . . . . . . . . . . . . . . . . . . . . . . . . . . . . . . . . . . . . . . . . . . . . . . . . . . . . . . . .
. . . . . . . . . . . . . . . . . . . . . . . . . . . . . . . . . . . . . . . . . . . . . . . . . . . . . . . . . . . . . . . . . . . . . . . . . . .
. . . . . . . . . . . . . . . . . . . . . . . . . . . . . . . . . . . . . . . . . . . . . . . . . . . . . . . . . . . . . . . . . . . . . . . . . . .
. . . . . . . . . . . . . . . . . . . . . . . . . . . . . . . . . . . . . . . . . . . . . . . . . . . . . . . . . . . . . . . . . . . . . . . . . . .
. . . . . . . . . . . . . . . . . . . . . . . . . . . . . . . . . . . . . . . . . . . . . . . . . . . . . . . . . . . . . . . . . . . . . . . . . . .
. . . . . . . . . . . . . . . . . . . . . . . . . . . . . . . . . . . . . . . . . . . . . . . . . . . . . . . . . . . . . . . . . . . . . . . . . . .
. . . . . . . . . . . . . . . . . . . . . . . . . . . . . . . . . . . . . . . . . . . . . . . . . . . . . . . . . . . . . . . . . . . . . . . . . . .
. . . . . . . . . . . . . . . . . . . . . . . . . . . . . . . . . . . . . . . . . . . . . . . . . . . . . . . . . . . . . . . . . . . . . . . . . . .

*Ten Weeks Old*

As you lie on your blanket, waving your hands and feet and trying to understand your fingers and toes, you give me such pleasure, Child! You gurgle deep in your throat and then light up with such a wide, toothless grin that I have to grin, too. I touch your cheek, ruffle your fuzzy hair, and love you so much it makes me shiver.

We adults like to think of ourselves as very grown up. But guess what, Little One? I suspect that when we are at our most serious—involved in our deepest discussions, proudest of our physical achievements, congratulating ourselves on our latest success—we are actually as amusing to our heavenly Parent as you are to me just now, lying there so intent on catching that sunbeam.

Why did God choose to create people in his own image? We don't know. But I hope that God gets as much pleasure from watching us as I get from watching you.

> **T**hen God said, "Let us make [human beings] in our image."
>
> GENESIS 1:26

## MY THOUGHTS, FEELINGS, AND PRAYERS FOR MY BABY

# Three
# Months Old

Tonight was dark and stormy, and we had to attend a large meeting. You did your best to smile at the strangers, but finally you began to fret. You were tired, and the room was much too bright and noisy.

At last I took you over near the fire and rocked you quietly. There, surrounded by thunder, lightning, and people noise, you turned your cheek to me and fell peacefully asleep.

Adults have times, too, Little One, when the hustle and bustle of life overwhelm them. We, too, get fretful and anxious. But as I watch you lie with complete abandon in my lap, sleeping the trusting sleep of infancy amid the chaos, I remember Jesus asleep in a boat on a storm-tossed sea. I remember that God has promised to keep us safe at all times in his everlasting arms.

I forget that message too often, My Child. Thank you for reminding me that when life gets stormy and crowded, I, too, have a safe place on the lap of my heavenly Parent.

**Do** not let
your hearts
be troubled.
Trust in God;
trust also in me.

JOHN 14:1

## My Thoughts, Feelings, and Prayers for My Baby

......................................................
......................................................
......................................................
......................................................
......................................................
......................................................
......................................................
......................................................
......................................................
......................................................
......................................................
......................................................
......................................................
......................................................
......................................................
......................................................
......................................................
......................................................
......................................................
......................................................
......................................................
......................................................

# Four Months Old

This morning as I lifted you from your crib to your swing and dangled your rag doll until you chortled with glee, I wondered if that child Jesus blessed could have been as little as you. If so, was Jesus reminding us how dependent we are on our heavenly Parent?

We adults take pride in our independence, our self-sufficiency. But the truth is, Little One, we can no more move into tomorrow without God than you can move alone from your bed to your swing. We depend more on God for our next breath than you depend on me for your next meal.

The difference between adults and infants is that you don't mind being dependent. You have no hang-ups about asking for and receiving my help. You call me when you need me and reward me for my assistance with grins and giggles.

Sometimes I insist on being independent when I don't feel it because I hate to ask anyone for help—even God. But I'm not always as independent as I like to pretend I am. Sometimes I really do need help. Thank you, Child, for showing me that there's nothing the matter with asking for help.

> **I tell you the truth, anyone who will not receive the kingdom of God like a little child will never enter it.**
>
> MARK 10:15

## My Thoughts, Feelings, and Prayers for My Baby

. . . . . . . . . . . . . . . . . . . . . . . . . . . . . . . . . . . . . . . . . . . . . . . . . . . . . . . .

. . . . . . . . . . . . . . . . . . . . . . . . . . . . . . . . . . . . . . . . . . . . . . . . . . . . . . . .

. . . . . . . . . . . . . . . . . . . . . . . . . . . . . . . . . . . . . . . . . . . . . . . . . . . . . . . .

. . . . . . . . . . . . . . . . . . . . . . . . . . . . . . . . . . . . . . . . . . . . . . . . . . . . . . . .

. . . . . . . . . . . . . . . . . . . . . . . . . . . . . . . . . . . . . . . . . . . . . . . . . . . . . . . .

. . . . . . . . . . . . . . . . . . . . . . . . . . . . . . . . . . . . . . . . . . . . . . . . . . . . . . . .

. . . . . . . . . . . . . . . . . . . . . . . . . . . . . . . . . . . . . . . . . . . . . . . . . . . . . . . .

. . . . . . . . . . . . . . . . . . . . . . . . . . . . . . . . . . . . . . . . . . . . . . . . . . . . . . . .

. . . . . . . . . . . . . . . . . . . . . . . . . . . . . . . . . . . . . . . . . . . . . . . . . . . . . . . .

. . . . . . . . . . . . . . . . . . . . . . . . . . . . . . . . . . . . . . . . . . . . . . . . . . . . . . . .

. . . . . . . . . . . . . . . . . . . . . . . . . . . . . . . . . . . . . . . . . . . . . . . . . . . . . . . .

. . . . . . . . . . . . . . . . . . . . . . . . . . . . . . . . . . . . . . . . . . . . . . . . . . . . . . . .

. . . . . . . . . . . . . . . . . . . . . . . . . . . . . . . . . . . . . . . . . . . . . . . . . . . . . . . .

. . . . . . . . . . . . . . . . . . . . . . . . . . . . . . . . . . . . . . . . . . . . . . . . . . . . . . . .

. . . . . . . . . . . . . . . . . . . . . . . . . . . . . . . . . . . . . . . . . . . . . . . . . . . . . . . .

. . . . . . . . . . . . . . . . . . . . . . . . . . . . . . . . . . . . . . . . . . . . . . . . . . . . . . . .

. . . . . . . . . . . . . . . . . . . . . . . . . . . . . . . . . . . . . . . . . . . . . . . . . . . . . . . .

. . . . . . . . . . . . . . . . . . . . . . . . . . . . . . . . . . . . . . . . . . . . . . . . . . . . . . . .

# Five
## Months Old

**H**ow you stretch my world, Little One!

Just having you in my arms brings strangers to my side, and we become sisters in the mystery that is motherhood. One tells me of her hard labor, and we commiserate as we share stories of pain. Another speaks of her child's ear infection, and we share worries over our babies' health. A third shyly says, "What a lovely baby," and joy floods her face as I reply, "And your little boy is so strong!"

What does it matter that we do not know one another's names, that we vote differently, that our bank accounts are as different as our ethnic backgrounds? What matters is that we have something important in common: our babies.

As I push you home from the park, I think that motherhood is very like the family of God. Why do I spend so much time noticing my differences from other Christians? All that really matters is that we have something important in common: our love for Jesus.

38

## My Thoughts, Feelings, and Prayers for My Baby

. . . . . . . . . . . . . . . . . . . . . . . . . . . . . . . . . . . . . . . . . . . . . . . . . . . . . . . . . . . . . . . . . . . . . . . . . . . . . . . . . . . . . .

. . . . . . . . . . . . . . . . . . . . . . . . . . . . . . . . . . . . . . . . . . . . . . . . . . . . . . . . . . . . . . . . . . . . . . . . . . . . . . . . . . . . . .

. . . . . . . . . . . . . . . . . . . . . . . . . . . . . . . . . . . . . . . . . . . . . . . . . . . . . . . . . . . . . . . . . . . . . . . . . . . . . . . . . . . . . .

. . . . . . . . . . . . . . . . . . . . . . . . . . . . . . . . . . . . . . . . . . . . . . . . . . . . . . . . . . . . . . . . . . . . . . . . . . . . . . . . . . . . . .

. . . . . . . . . . . . . . . . . . . . . . . . . . . . . . . . . . . . . . . . . . . . . . . . . . . . . . . . . . . . . . . . . . . . . . . . . . . . . . . . . . . . . .

. . . . . . . . . . . . . . . . . . . . . . . . . . . . . . . . . . . . . . . . . . . . . . . . . . . . . . . . . . . . . . . . . . . . . . . . . . . . . . . . . . . . . .

. . . . . . . . . . . . . . . . . . . . . . . . . . . . . . . . . . . . . . . . . . . . . . . . . . . . . . . . . . . . . . . . . . . . . . . . . . . . . . . . . . . . . .

. . . . . . . . . . . . . . . . . . . . . . . . . . . . . . . . . . . . . . . . . . . . . . . . . . . . . . . . . . . . . . . . . . . . . . . . . . . . . . . . . . . . . .

. . . . . . . . . . . . . . . . . . . . . . . . . . . . . . . . . . . . . . . . . . . . . . . . . . . . . . . . . . . . . . . . . . . . . . . . . . . . . . . . . . . . . .

. . . . . . . . . . . . . . . . . . . . . . . . . . . . . . . . . . . . . . . . . . . . . . . . . . . . . . . . . . . . . . . . . . . . . . . . . . . . . . . . . . . . . .

. . . . . . . . . . . . . . . . . . . . . . . . . . . . . . . . . . . . . . . . . . . . . . . . . . . . . . . . . . . . . . . . . . . . . . . . . . . . . . . . . . . . . .

. . . . . . . . . . . . . . . . . . . . . . . . . . . . . . . . . . . . . . . . . . . . . . . . . . . . . . . . . . . . . . . . . . . . . . . . . . . . . . . . . . . . . .

. . . . . . . . . . . . . . . . . . . . . . . . . . . . . . . . . . . . . . . . . . . . . . . . . . . . . . . . . . . . . . . . . . . . . . . . . . . . . . . . . . . . . .

. . . . . . . . . . . . . . . . . . . . . . . . . . . . . . . . . . . . . . . . . . . . . . . . . . . . . . . . . . . . . . . . . . . . . . . . . . . . . . . . . . . . . .

. . . . . . . . . . . . . . . . . . . . . . . . . . . . . . . . . . . . . . . . . . . . . . . . . . . . . . . . . . . . . . . . . . . . . . . . . . . . . . . . . . . . . .

. . . . . . . . . . . . . . . . . . . . . . . . . . . . . . . . . . . . . . . . . . . . . . . . . . . . . . . . . . . . . . . . . . . . . . . . . . . . . . . . . . . . . .

. . . . . . . . . . . . . . . . . . . . . . . . . . . . . . . . . . . . . . . . . . . . . . . . . . . . . . . . . . . . . . . . . . . . . . . . . . . . . . . . . . . . . .

. . . . . . . . . . . . . . . . . . . . . . . . . . . . . . . . . . . . . . . . . . . . . . . . . . . . . . . . . . . . . . . . . . . . . . . . . . . . . . . . . . . . . .

. . . . . . . . . . . . . . . . . . . . . . . . . . . . . . . . . . . . . . . . . . . . . . . . . . . . . . . . . . . . . . . . . . . . . . . . . . . . . . . . . . . . . .

# Six Months Old

**P**oor little baby. You desperately want to crawl, but your arms and legs won't obey. Every time you lurch toward your red ball, you find that instead you have somehow backed farther away from it. How furious you are!

If only I could make you understand that you are doing fine. Going backward is your first step in going forward, Little One. At least you are now moving. Last week you couldn't even do that. Don't you see how proud Mama and Daddy are of you?

No, all you can see is that red ball, moving farther away. You don't realize that the process you are going through is much more important than that silly ball.

Watching you makes me wonder how often I am just like you. I think I am succeeding in my walk of faith; then something happens and I fail. "I'm going backward," I wail, furious with myself.

But watching you today, I remember how often I learn good lessons from my failures. I begin to wonder. Is it possible that times that look to me like failures are just another part of God's faith-growth process?

> **F**or in him
> we live
> and move
> and have our being.
>
> ACTS 17:28

## My Thoughts, Feelings, and Prayers for My Baby

## Six-and-One-Half Months Old

**H**ush, Baby, Mama's right here. I only stepped into the yard for a few minutes to bring in your clothes from the line. Lately, every time I am out of sight you get worried. Trust me, Beloved. I'll be right back.

I wonder if that's why the Bible says, "Don't be afraid," so often. We can't always see what God is doing for us. Sometimes he seems to have disappeared, and we feel so lonely, so abandoned.

But listen! There's a voice even in dark and lonely times, a voice that says gently, "Trust me, Beloved. I'll be right back."

## My Thoughts, Feelings, and Prayers for My Baby

. . . . . . . . . . . . . . . . . . . . . . . . . . . . . . . . . . . . . . . . . . . . . . . . . . . . . . . . . . . . . . . . . . . . . . . . . . . . . . . . . . . . . . . . . . . . . . . .

. . . . . . . . . . . . . . . . . . . . . . . . . . . . . . . . . . . . . . . . . . . . . . . . . . . . . . . . . . . . . . . . . . . . . . . . . . . . . . . . . . . . . . . . . . . . . . . .

. . . . . . . . . . . . . . . . . . . . . . . . . . . . . . . . . . . . . . . . . . . . . . . . . . . . . . . . . . . . . . . . . . . . . . . . . . . . . . . . . . . . . . . . . . . . . . . .

. . . . . . . . . . . . . . . . . . . . . . . . . . . . . . . . . . . . . . . . . . . . . . . . . . . . . . . . . . . . . . . . . . . . . . . . . . . . . . . . . . . . . . . . . . . . . . . .

. . . . . . . . . . . . . . . . . . . . . . . . . . . . . . . . . . . . . . . . . . . . . . . . . . . . . . . . . . . . . . . . . . . . . . . . . . . . . . . . . . . . . . . . . . . . . . . .

. . . . . . . . . . . . . . . . . . . . . . . . . . . . . . . . . . . . . . . . . . . . . . . . . . . . . . . . . . . . . . . . . . . . . . . . . . . . . . . . . . . . . . . . . . . . . . . .

. . . . . . . . . . . . . . . . . . . . . . . . . . . . . . . . . . . . . . . . . . . . . . . . . . . . . . . . . . . . . . . . . . . . . . . . . . . . . . . . . . . . . . . . . . . . . . . .

. . . . . . . . . . . . . . . . . . . . . . . . . . . . . . . . . . . . . . . . . . . . . . . . . . . . . . . . . . . . . . . . . . . . . . . . . . . . . . . . . . . . . . . . . . . . . . . .

. . . . . . . . . . . . . . . . . . . . . . . . . . . . . . . . . . . . . . . . . . . . . . . . . . . . . . . . . . . . . . . . . . . . . . . . . . . . . . . . . . . . . . . . . . . . . . . .

. . . . . . . . . . . . . . . . . . . . . . . . . . . . . . . . . . . . . . . . . . . . . . . . . . . . . . . . . . . . . . . . . . . . . . . . . . . . . . . . . . . . . . . . . . . . . . . .

. . . . . . . . . . . . . . . . . . . . . . . . . . . . . . . . . . . . . . . . . . . . . . . . . . . . . . . . . . . . . . . . . . . . . . . . . . . . . . . . . . . . . . . . . . . . . . . .

. . . . . . . . . . . . . . . . . . . . . . . . . . . . . . . . . . . . . . . . . . . . . . . . . . . . . . . . . . . . . . . . . . . . . . . . . . . . . . . . . . . . . . . . . . . . . . . .

. . . . . . . . . . . . . . . . . . . . . . . . . . . . . . . . . . . . . . . . . . . . . . . . . . . . . . . . . . . . . . . . . . . . . . . . . . . . . . . . . . . . . . . . . . . . . . . .

. . . . . . . . . . . . . . . . . . . . . . . . . . . . . . . . . . . . . . . . . . . . . . . . . . . . . . . . . . . . . . . . . . . . . . . . . . . . . . . . . . . . . . . . . . . . . . . .

. . . . . . . . . . . . . . . . . . . . . . . . . . . . . . . . . . . . . . . . . . . . . . . . . . . . . . . . . . . . . . . . . . . . . . . . . . . . . . . . . . . . . . . . . . . . . . . .

. . . . . . . . . . . . . . . . . . . . . . . . . . . . . . . . . . . . . . . . . . . . . . . . . . . . . . . . . . . . . . . . . . . . . . . . . . . . . . . . . . . . . . . . . . . . . . . .

. . . . . . . . . . . . . . . . . . . . . . . . . . . . . . . . . . . . . . . . . . . . . . . . . . . . . . . . . . . . . . . . . . . . . . . . . . . . . . . . . . . . . . . . . . . . . . . .

. . . . . . . . . . . . . . . . . . . . . . . . . . . . . . . . . . . . . . . . . . . . . . . . . . . . . . . . . . . . . . . . . . . . . . . . . . . . . . . . . . . . . . . . . . . . . . . .

. . . . . . . . . . . . . . . . . . . . . . . . . . . . . . . . . . . . . . . . . . . . . . . . . . . . . . . . . . . . . . . . . . . . . . . . . . . . . . . . . . . . . . . . . . . . . . . .

. . . . . . . . . . . . . . . . . . . . . . . . . . . . . . . . . . . . . . . . . . . . . . . . . . . . . . . . . . . . . . . . . . . . . . . . . . . . . . . . . . . . . . . . . . . . . . . .

. . . . . . . . . . . . . . . . . . . . . . . . . . . . . . . . . . . . . . . . . . . . . . . . . . . . . . . . . . . . . . . . . . . . . . . . . . . . . . . . . . . . . . . . . . . . . . . .

. . . . . . . . . . . . . . . . . . . . . . . . . . . . . . . . . . . . . . . . . . . . . . . . . . . . . . . . . . . . . . . . . . . . . . . . . . . . . . . . . . . . . . . . . . . . . . . .

## *Seven Months Old*

**Even the very hairs of your head are all numbered.**

<small>MATTHEW 10:30</small>

ou lie beside me on the bed while I read. You are awake, but you are not yet alert. You give me an adoring smile and stare at me intently, memorizing my face.

"Counting my freckles?" I tease, reaching over to tickle your tummy. You chortle and grab my hair, giving it a gentle tug.

I remember something Jesus said: God has counted every hair on my head.

When you were looking at me just now, your eyes reflected the very love of God.

## MY THOUGHTS, FEELINGS, AND PRAYERS FOR MY BABY

. . . . . . . . . . . . . . . . . . . . . . . . . . . . . . . . . . . . . . . . . . . . . . . . . . . . . . . . . . . . . . . . . . . . . . . . . . . . . .

. . . . . . . . . . . . . . . . . . . . . . . . . . . . . . . . . . . . . . . . . . . . . . . . . . . . . . . . . . . . . . . . . . . . . . . . . . . . . .

. . . . . . . . . . . . . . . . . . . . . . . . . . . . . . . . . . . . . . . . . . . . . . . . . . . . . . . . . . . . . . . . . . . . . . . . . . . . . .

. . . . . . . . . . . . . . . . . . . . . . . . . . . . . . . . . . . . . . . . . . . . . . . . . . . . . . . . . . . . . . . . . . . . . . . . . . . . . .

. . . . . . . . . . . . . . . . . . . . . . . . . . . . . . . . . . . . . . . . . . . . . . . . . . . . . . . . . . . . . . . . . . . . . . . . . . . . . .

. . . . . . . . . . . . . . . . . . . . . . . . . . . . . . . . . . . . . . . . . . . . . . . . . . . . . . . . . . . . . . . . . . . . . . . . . . . . . .

. . . . . . . . . . . . . . . . . . . . . . . . . . . . . . . . . . . . . . . . . . . . . . . . . . . . . . . . . . . . . . . . . . . . . . . . . . . . . .

. . . . . . . . . . . . . . . . . . . . . . . . . . . . . . . . . . . . . . . . . . . . . . . . . . . . . . . . . . . . . . . . . . . . . . . . . . . . . .

. . . . . . . . . . . . . . . . . . . . . . . . . . . . . . . . . . . . . . . . . . . . . . . . . . . . . . . . . . . . . . . . . . . . . . . . . . . . . .

. . . . . . . . . . . . . . . . . . . . . . . . . . . . . . . . . . . . . . . . . . . . . . . . . . . . . . . . . . . . . . . . . . . . . . . . . . . . . .

. . . . . . . . . . . . . . . . . . . . . . . . . . . . . . . . . . . . . . . . . . . . . . . . . . . . . . . . . . . . . . . . . . . . . . . . . . . . . .

. . . . . . . . . . . . . . . . . . . . . . . . . . . . . . . . . . . . . . . . . . . . . . . . . . . . . . . . . . . . . . . . . . . . . . . . . . . . . .

. . . . . . . . . . . . . . . . . . . . . . . . . . . . . . . . . . . . . . . . . . . . . . . . . . . . . . . . . . . . . . . . . . . . . . . . . . . . . .

. . . . . . . . . . . . . . . . . . . . . . . . . . . . . . . . . . . . . . . . . . . . . . . . . . . . . . . . . . . . . . . . . . . . . . . . . . . . . .

. . . . . . . . . . . . . . . . . . . . . . . . . . . . . . . . . . . . . . . . . . . . . . . . . . . . . . . . . . . . . . . . . . . . . . . . . . . . . .

. . . . . . . . . . . . . . . . . . . . . . . . . . . . . . . . . . . . . . . . . . . . . . . . . . . . . . . . . . . . . . . . . . . . . . . . . . . . . .

. . . . . . . . . . . . . . . . . . . . . . . . . . . . . . . . . . . . . . . . . . . . . . . . . . . . . . . . . . . . . . . . . . . . . . . . . . . . . .

# Seven-and-One-Half-Months Old

**W**hich is grubbier, learning to crawl or learning to eat? Lately, you seem to need three baths a day!

But how you love those baths—splashing, letting droplets fall from your fingers, tasting the soap to see if it is better this time. You gurgle and coo and crow with delight as your yellow duck bobs out of reach.

I love the baths too—washing you and watching your soft skin emerge from the dirt or beets. Wrapping you in a fluffy towel, playing peek-a-boo, letting you lie naked to the world while you enjoy a gentle breeze. It's a good thing that bath times are so special, Little One, for we seem to have a lot of them lately.

Watching you in your bath reminds me of the way I feel after confessing my sins to God— clean, refreshed, and pounds lighter.

## MY THOUGHTS, FEELINGS, AND PRAYERS FOR MY BABY

....................................................................

....................................................................

....................................................................

....................................................................

....................................................................

....................................................................

....................................................................

....................................................................

....................................................................

....................................................................

....................................................................

....................................................................

....................................................................

....................................................................

....................................................................

....................................................................

....................................................................

....................................................................

....................................................................

....................................................................

# Eight Months Old

> **T**here is a time
> for everything,
> and a season
> for every activity
> under heaven.
>
> ECCLESIASTES 3:1

**T**oday while I prepared to shower, I put you in the playpen with some favorite toys and a brand new book. "Please give me ten minutes?" I asked. "Read your book."

Instead, you stood and clung to the rail, clamoring to be let out. "Silly child, it's only temporary," I called. But still you yelled.

And I've been doing the same thing this week, haven't I? Thinking of the freedom I had before you were born, freedom to meet a friend for lunch or eat pie in a restaurant with your daddy late at night. I have been whining and grumbling about being "stuck" at home with a baby (that's YOU!). When I could have been planting flowers, baking a cake, enjoying you, I've been standing at the screen door looking longingly up the road.

What's the matter with us, Child? Do we fear we'll be trapped in these playpens forever? Why can't we both see how temporary they are—and enjoy for now the playthings we've been given?

I'm coming to get you now. Let's go outside together.

## My Thoughts, Feelings, and Prayers for My Baby

. . . . . . . . . . . . . . . . . . . . . . . . . . . . . . . . . . . . . . . . . . . . . . . . . . . . . . . .

. . . . . . . . . . . . . . . . . . . . . . . . . . . . . . . . . . . . . . . . . . . . . . . . . . . . . . . .

. . . . . . . . . . . . . . . . . . . . . . . . . . . . . . . . . . . . . . . . . . . . . . . . . . . . . . . .

. . . . . . . . . . . . . . . . . . . . . . . . . . . . . . . . . . . . . . . . . . . . . . . . . . . . . . . .

. . . . . . . . . . . . . . . . . . . . . . . . . . . . . . . . . . . . . . . . . . . . . . . . . . . . . . . .

. . . . . . . . . . . . . . . . . . . . . . . . . . . . . . . . . . . . . . . . . . . . . . . . . . . . . . . .

. . . . . . . . . . . . . . . . . . . . . . . . . . . . . . . . . . . . . . . . . . . . . . . . . . . . . . . .

. . . . . . . . . . . . . . . . . . . . . . . . . . . . . . . . . . . . . . . . . . . . . . . . . . . . . . . .

. . . . . . . . . . . . . . . . . . . . . . . . . . . . . . . . . . . . . . . . . . . . . . . . . . . . . . . .

. . . . . . . . . . . . . . . . . . . . . . . . . . . . . . . . . . . . . . . . . . . . . . . . . . . . . . . .

. . . . . . . . . . . . . . . . . . . . . . . . . . . . . . . . . . . . . . . . . . . . . . . . . . . . . . . .

. . . . . . . . . . . . . . . . . . . . . . . . . . . . . . . . . . . . . . . . . . . . . . . . . . . . . . . .

. . . . . . . . . . . . . . . . . . . . . . . . . . . . . . . . . . . . . . . . . . . . . . . . . . . . . . . .

. . . . . . . . . . . . . . . . . . . . . . . . . . . . . . . . . . . . . . . . . . . . . . . . . . . . . . . .

. . . . . . . . . . . . . . . . . . . . . . . . . . . . . . . . . . . . . . . . . . . . . . . . . . . . . . . .

. . . . . . . . . . . . . . . . . . . . . . . . . . . . . . . . . . . . . . . . . . . . . . . . . . . . . . . .

. . . . . . . . . . . . . . . . . . . . . . . . . . . . . . . . . . . . . . . . . . . . . . . . . . . . . . . .

. . . . . . . . . . . . . . . . . . . . . . . . . . . . . . . . . . . . . . . . . . . . . . . . . . . . . . . .

. . . . . . . . . . . . . . . . . . . . . . . . . . . . . . . . . . . . . . . . . . . . . . . . . . . . . . . .

. . . . . . . . . . . . . . . . . . . . . . . . . . . . . . . . . . . . . . . . . . . . . . . . . . . . . . . .

. . . . . . . . . . . . . . . . . . . . . . . . . . . . . . . . . . . . . . . . . . . . . . . . . . . . . . . .

# Eight-and-One-Half Months Old

Some days what I do for you seems so repetitive, so trivial. As I heat jars of baby food, find yet another outfit to replace the third one you've dirtied today, or read your favorite book for the second time in an hour, I wonder if anything I do for you is *really* important.

Then you fall: Bump! It isn't much, a tiny cut. But when a drop of blood oozes out, you begin to roar: "Mama, Mama!" Tears streaming down your cheeks, you hold it out for me to see.

Solemnly we apply a dab of antiseptic, a colorful bandage. Then I scoop you up, still hiccuping, and carry you out for a cuddle on the grass.

A yellow and black butterfly lands near us, and your eyes sparkle behind their tears. "Puk, puk," you gurgle.

"Bug," I agree. And we share a hug and a laugh.

Much of what I do for you seems trivial, Little One. But when I am there to share your sorrows and your joys, that's very important indeed!

> **R**ejoice with those who rejoice; mourn with those who mourn.
>
> ROMANS 12:15

## My Thoughts, Feelings, and Prayers for My Baby

. . . . . . . . . . . . . . . . . . . . . . . . . . . . . . . . . . . . . . . . . . . . . . . . . . . . . . . . . . . . . . . . . . . .

. . . . . . . . . . . . . . . . . . . . . . . . . . . . . . . . . . . . . . . . . . . . . . . . . . . . . . . . . . . . . . . . . . . .

. . . . . . . . . . . . . . . . . . . . . . . . . . . . . . . . . . . . . . . . . . . . . . . . . . . . . . . . . . . . . . . . . . . .

. . . . . . . . . . . . . . . . . . . . . . . . . . . . . . . . . . . . . . . . . . . . . . . . . . . . . . . . . . . . . . . . . . . .

. . . . . . . . . . . . . . . . . . . . . . . . . . . . . . . . . . . . . . . . . . . . . . . . . . . . . . . . . . . . . . . . . . . .

. . . . . . . . . . . . . . . . . . . . . . . . . . . . . . . . . . . . . . . . . . . . . . . . . . . . . . . . . . . . . . . . . . . .

. . . . . . . . . . . . . . . . . . . . . . . . . . . . . . . . . . . . . . . . . . . . . . . . . . . . . . . . . . . . . . . . . . . .

. . . . . . . . . . . . . . . . . . . . . . . . . . . . . . . . . . . . . . . . . . . . . . . . . . . . . . . . . . . . . . . . . . . .

. . . . . . . . . . . . . . . . . . . . . . . . . . . . . . . . . . . . . . . . . . . . . . . . . . . . . . . . . . . . . . . . . . . .

. . . . . . . . . . . . . . . . . . . . . . . . . . . . . . . . . . . . . . . . . . . . . . . . . . . . . . . . . . . . . . . . . . . .

. . . . . . . . . . . . . . . . . . . . . . . . . . . . . . . . . . . . . . . . . . . . . . . . . . . . . . . . . . . . . . . . . . . .

. . . . . . . . . . . . . . . . . . . . . . . . . . . . . . . . . . . . . . . . . . . . . . . . . . . . . . . . . . . . . . . . . . . .

. . . . . . . . . . . . . . . . . . . . . . . . . . . . . . . . . . . . . . . . . . . . . . . . . . . . . . . . . . . . . . . . . . . .

. . . . . . . . . . . . . . . . . . . . . . . . . . . . . . . . . . . . . . . . . . . . . . . . . . . . . . . . . . . . . . . . . . . .

. . . . . . . . . . . . . . . . . . . . . . . . . . . . . . . . . . . . . . . . . . . . . . . . . . . . . . . . . . . . . . . . . . . .

. . . . . . . . . . . . . . . . . . . . . . . . . . . . . . . . . . . . . . . . . . . . . . . . . . . . . . . . . . . . . . . . . . . .

. . . . . . . . . . . . . . . . . . . . . . . . . . . . . . . . . . . . . . . . . . . . . . . . . . . . . . . . . . . . . . . . . . . .

. . . . . . . . . . . . . . . . . . . . . . . . . . . . . . . . . . . . . . . . . . . . . . . . . . . . . . . . . . . . . . . . . . . .

. . . . . . . . . . . . . . . . . . . . . . . . . . . . . . . . . . . . . . . . . . . . . . . . . . . . . . . . . . . . . . . . . . . .

. . . . . . . . . . . . . . . . . . . . . . . . . . . . . . . . . . . . . . . . . . . . . . . . . . . . . . . . . . . . . . . . . . . .

**Y**ou stand under the kitchen table beside my knees and roar. You want to come up onto my lap, but you bump your head every time you try. "Bow your head and bend your knees," I urge. I put my hand on your head and try to gently press you down a little.

But you don't want to bow your head nor bend your knees. So there you stand—unbowed, unbent, unhappy.

I want to hold you, Little One, but there's no way for you to come up to me unless you bow your head and bend your knees. What a frustrating situation.

You remind me of myself when I feel separated from God and know it's because of something I've done, or something he wants me to do that I'm unwilling to do. I don't want to bow my head and bend my knees to him either.

Why are you so stubborn, I wonder? Can't you see I am waiting? Suddenly you catch on. Carefully you bend and bow, take one hesitant step and I catch you before you fall.

Why am I so stubborn, I wonder? My Father is waiting.

**At the name
of Jesus
every knee
should bow.**

PHILIPPIANS 2:10

## MY THOUGHTS, FEELINGS, AND PRAYERS FOR MY BABY

. . . . . . . . . . . . . . . . . . . . . . . . . . . . . . . . . . . . . . . . . . . . . . . . . . . . . . . . . . . . . . . . . . . . . . . . . . . . . . . . . . . . . . . . . . . . . . . . . . . . . . . . . . . . . .

. . . . . . . . . . . . . . . . . . . . . . . . . . . . . . . . . . . . . . . . . . . . . . . . . . . . . . . . . . . . . . . . . . . . . . . . . . . . . . . . . . . . . . . . . . . . . . . . . . . . . . . . . . . . . .

. . . . . . . . . . . . . . . . . . . . . . . . . . . . . . . . . . . . . . . . . . . . . . . . . . . . . . . . . . . . . . . . . . . . . . . . . . . . . . . . . . . . . . . . . . . . . . . . . . . . . . . . . . . . . .

. . . . . . . . . . . . . . . . . . . . . . . . . . . . . . . . . . . . . . . . . . . . . . . . . . . . . . . . . . . . . . . . . . . . . . . . . . . . . . . . . . . . . . . . . . . . . . . . . . . . . . . . . . . . . .

. . . . . . . . . . . . . . . . . . . . . . . . . . . . . . . . . . . . . . . . . . . . . . . . . . . . . . . . . . . . . . . . . . . . . . . . . . . . . . . . . . . . . . . . . . . . . . . . . . . . . . . . . . . . . .

. . . . . . . . . . . . . . . . . . . . . . . . . . . . . . . . . . . . . . . . . . . . . . . . . . . . . . . . . . . . . . . . . . . . . . . . . . . . . . . . . . . . . . . . . . . . . . . . . . . . . . . . . . . . . .

. . . . . . . . . . . . . . . . . . . . . . . . . . . . . . . . . . . . . . . . . . . . . . . . . . . . . . . . . . . . . . . . . . . . . . . . . . . . . . . . . . . . . . . . . . . . . . . . . . . . . . . . . . . . . .

. . . . . . . . . . . . . . . . . . . . . . . . . . . . . . . . . . . . . . . . . . . . . . . . . . . . . . . . . . . . . . . . . . . . . . . . . . . . . . . . . . . . . . . . . . . . . . . . . . . . . . . . . . . . . .

. . . . . . . . . . . . . . . . . . . . . . . . . . . . . . . . . . . . . . . . . . . . . . . . . . . . . . . . . . . . . . . . . . . . . . . . . . . . . . . . . . . . . . . . . . . . . . . . . . . . . . . . . . . . . .

. . . . . . . . . . . . . . . . . . . . . . . . . . . . . . . . . . . . . . . . . . . . . . . . . . . . . . . . . . . . . . . . . . . . . . . . . . . . . . . . . . . . . . . . . . . . . . . . . . . . . . . . . . . . . .

. . . . . . . . . . . . . . . . . . . . . . . . . . . . . . . . . . . . . . . . . . . . . . . . . . . . . . . . . . . . . . . . . . . . . . . . . . . . . . . . . . . . . . . . . . . . . . . . . . . . . . . . . . . . . .

. . . . . . . . . . . . . . . . . . . . . . . . . . . . . . . . . . . . . . . . . . . . . . . . . . . . . . . . . . . . . . . . . . . . . . . . . . . . . . . . . . . . . . . . . . . . . . . . . . . . . . . . . . . . . .

. . . . . . . . . . . . . . . . . . . . . . . . . . . . . . . . . . . . . . . . . . . . . . . . . . . . . . . . . . . . . . . . . . . . . . . . . . . . . . . . . . . . . . . . . . . . . . . . . . . . . . . . . . . . . .

. . . . . . . . . . . . . . . . . . . . . . . . . . . . . . . . . . . . . . . . . . . . . . . . . . . . . . . . . . . . . . . . . . . . . . . . . . . . . . . . . . . . . . . . . . . . . . . . . . . . . . . . . . . . . .

. . . . . . . . . . . . . . . . . . . . . . . . . . . . . . . . . . . . . . . . . . . . . . . . . . . . . . . . . . . . . . . . . . . . . . . . . . . . . . . . . . . . . . . . . . . . . . . . . . . . . . . . . . . . . .

. . . . . . . . . . . . . . . . . . . . . . . . . . . . . . . . . . . . . . . . . . . . . . . . . . . . . . . . . . . . . . . . . . . . . . . . . . . . . . . . . . . . . . . . . . . . . . . . . . . . . . . . . . . . . .

. . . . . . . . . . . . . . . . . . . . . . . . . . . . . . . . . . . . . . . . . . . . . . . . . . . . . . . . . . . . . . . . . . . . . . . . . . . . . . . . . . . . . . . . . . . . . . . . . . . . . . . . . . . . . .

. . . . . . . . . . . . . . . . . . . . . . . . . . . . . . . . . . . . . . . . . . . . . . . . . . . . . . . . . . . . . . . . . . . . . . . . . . . . . . . . . . . . . . . . . . . . . . . . . . . . . . . . . . . . . .

. . . . . . . . . . . . . . . . . . . . . . . . . . . . . . . . . . . . . . . . . . . . . . . . . . . . . . . . . . . . . . . . . . . . . . . . . . . . . . . . . . . . . . . . . . . . . . . . . . . . . . . . . . . . . .

. . . . . . . . . . . . . . . . . . . . . . . . . . . . . . . . . . . . . . . . . . . . . . . . . . . . . . . . . . . . . . . . . . . . . . . . . . . . . . . . . . . . . . . . . . . . . . . . . . . . . . . . . . . . . .

## Nine-and-One-Half Months Old

**H**ow delighted you are with yourself! Having mastered a chair, you now want to scale the table. Every day you have to explore each piece of furniture to see what new abilities you have acquired since yesterday. And you are having such fun.

When did I lose that self-delight? What happened to my awareness that every day I can do some things I have never been able to do before? What made me content to stop trying out yesterday's impossibilities to see if they could be done today?

Does being grown up mean being content with "what is" when we could be striving for "what could be"? Inspire me, Child, to stretch my world as you stretch yours.

## My Thoughts, Feelings, and Prayers for My Baby

.............................................................................

.............................................................................

.............................................................................

.............................................................................

.............................................................................

.............................................................................

.............................................................................

.............................................................................

.............................................................................

.............................................................................

.............................................................................

.............................................................................

.............................................................................

.............................................................................

.............................................................................

.............................................................................

.............................................................................

.............................................................................

.............................................................................

.............................................................................

.............................................................................

# Ten
# Months Old

> **W**e do not know
> what we ought
> to pray for,
> but the Spirit himself
> intercedes for us with
> groans that words
> cannot express.
>
> ROMANS 8:26

**Y**ou sure talk a lot, Little One. A strange language spoken only by babies. Sometimes you are so frustrated by people's inability to comprehend that you fall back to pointing a finger and saying, "uh-uh-uh!"

Don't worry. Most of the time we know what you want. We know you, you see, so we can translate.

Today I read in Romans that the Holy Spirit does the very same thing. When my prayers get bogged down in feelings I just don't know how to express, the Spirit will interpret them for me.

I guess all loving parents are good translators!

## My Thoughts, Feelings, and Prayers for My Baby

. . . . . . . . . . . . . . . . . . . . . . . . . . . . . . . . . . . . . . . . . . . . . . . . . . . . . . . . . . . . . . . . . . . . .

. . . . . . . . . . . . . . . . . . . . . . . . . . . . . . . . . . . . . . . . . . . . . . . . . . . . . . . . . . . . . . . . . . . . .

. . . . . . . . . . . . . . . . . . . . . . . . . . . . . . . . . . . . . . . . . . . . . . . . . . . . . . . . . . . . . . . . . . . . .

. . . . . . . . . . . . . . . . . . . . . . . . . . . . . . . . . . . . . . . . . . . . . . . . . . . . . . . . . . . . . . . . . . . . .

. . . . . . . . . . . . . . . . . . . . . . . . . . . . . . . . . . . . . . . . . . . . . . . . . . . . . . . . . . . . . . . . . . . . .

. . . . . . . . . . . . . . . . . . . . . . . . . . . . . . . . . . . . . . . . . . . . . . . . . . . . . . . . . . . . . . . . . . . . .

. . . . . . . . . . . . . . . . . . . . . . . . . . . . . . . . . . . . . . . . . . . . . . . . . . . . . . . . . . . . . . . . . . . . .

. . . . . . . . . . . . . . . . . . . . . . . . . . . . . . . . . . . . . . . . . . . . . . . . . . . . . . . . . . . . . . . . . . . . .

. . . . . . . . . . . . . . . . . . . . . . . . . . . . . . . . . . . . . . . . . . . . . . . . . . . . . . . . . . . . . . . . . . . . .

. . . . . . . . . . . . . . . . . . . . . . . . . . . . . . . . . . . . . . . . . . . . . . . . . . . . . . . . . . . . . . . . . . . . .

. . . . . . . . . . . . . . . . . . . . . . . . . . . . . . . . . . . . . . . . . . . . . . . . . . . . . . . . . . . . . . . . . . . . .

. . . . . . . . . . . . . . . . . . . . . . . . . . . . . . . . . . . . . . . . . . . . . . . . . . . . . . . . . . . . . . . . . . . . .

. . . . . . . . . . . . . . . . . . . . . . . . . . . . . . . . . . . . . . . . . . . . . . . . . . . . . . . . . . . . . . . . . . . . .

. . . . . . . . . . . . . . . . . . . . . . . . . . . . . . . . . . . . . . . . . . . . . . . . . . . . . . . . . . . . . . . . . . . . .

. . . . . . . . . . . . . . . . . . . . . . . . . . . . . . . . . . . . . . . . . . . . . . . . . . . . . . . . . . . . . . . . . . . . .

. . . . . . . . . . . . . . . . . . . . . . . . . . . . . . . . . . . . . . . . . . . . . . . . . . . . . . . . . . . . . . . . . . . . .

. . . . . . . . . . . . . . . . . . . . . . . . . . . . . . . . . . . . . . . . . . . . . . . . . . . . . . . . . . . . . . . . . . . . .

. . . . . . . . . . . . . . . . . . . . . . . . . . . . . . . . . . . . . . . . . . . . . . . . . . . . . . . . . . . . . . . . . . . . .

. . . . . . . . . . . . . . . . . . . . . . . . . . . . . . . . . . . . . . . . . . . . . . . . . . . . . . . . . . . . . . . . . . . . .

. . . . . . . . . . . . . . . . . . . . . . . . . . . . . . . . . . . . . . . . . . . . . . . . . . . . . . . . . . . . . . . . . . . . .

. . . . . . . . . . . . . . . . . . . . . . . . . . . . . . . . . . . . . . . . . . . . . . . . . . . . . . . . . . . . . . . . . . . . .

. . . . . . . . . . . . . . . . . . . . . . . . . . . . . . . . . . . . . . . . . . . . . . . . . . . . . . . . . . . . . . . . . . . . .

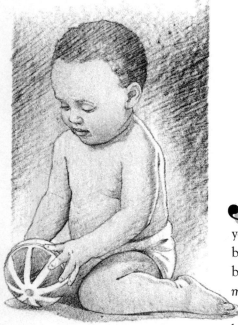

# Ten-and-One-Half Months Old

Silly Baby. You want to play ball, but you don't understand the rules. I can't catch the ball unless you throw it. So, you sit there with a bewildered expression. *Why won't she play with me?* you seem to be thinking.

But I can't play with you as long as you keep the ball. You have to trust me for a little while; roll the ball to me and count on me to return it. Then, we will have a marvelous game!

You remind me of myself when I clutch people or things and then wonder why they seem to slip from my grasp. Jesus pointed out that whatever we try to hold on to we will lose. We only get what we are willing to give away. When I am willing to relax my grasp and give something to him, he gives back far more than I gave.

O.K., Child, roll the ball, and we'll play a game!

> **W**hoever finds his life
> will lose it,
> and whoever loses
> his life for my sake
> will find it.
>
> MATTHEW 10:39

## My Thoughts, Feelings, and Prayers for My Baby

.................................................................
.................................................................
.................................................................
.................................................................
.................................................................
.................................................................
.................................................................
.................................................................
.................................................................
.................................................................
.................................................................
.................................................................
.................................................................
.................................................................
.................................................................
.................................................................
.................................................................
.................................................................
.................................................................
.................................................................
.................................................................

# Eleven Months Old

Some older boys dropped by to play with you this afternoon, and in their ten-year-old exuberance they were rough. You became apprehensive, then frightened. Finally you looked wildly around and wept. One of the boys reached down and picked you up. "Cut it out," he told the others. I could have hugged him.

I had been watching all the time, you see, aching to interfere. How I hate to see you frightened, hurt, or excluded by other children! But you must learn to live in this often cruel world, so I stood back for a time—and hurt. Until you were born, I never knew the intense pain of non-interfering love.

Now I look with different eyes when I see some of God's children being frightened, injured, or excluded by others. I used to think about the children's pain. Now I see with parent's eyes. Now I know a little of what God must suffer, too.

I marvel that he can watch as long as he does without interfering. How can he bear so much pain?

I know that I need to stand up for God's hurting children and say, "Cut it out!"

> **H**ow great is the love
> the Father has
> lavished on us, that we
> should be called
> children of God!
>
> 1 JOHN 3:1

## My Thoughts, Feelings, and Prayers for My Baby

................................................................
................................................................
................................................................
................................................................
................................................................
................................................................
................................................................
................................................................
................................................................
................................................................
................................................................
................................................................
................................................................
................................................................
................................................................
................................................................
................................................................
................................................................
................................................................
................................................................

# Eleven-and-One-Half Months Old

**W**hat a hectic week! With all this rain, we are both getting the cooped-up grumblies. This morning, while I was cleaning up the sugar you'd dumped on the kitchen floor, you were busily shredding tissues. While I was cleaning up the tissues, you were dusting the bathroom—and yourself—with my good bath powder. If you hadn't looked so cute, I would have cried.

Then a friend called with a proposal that I couldn't refuse. I'll take yours for the afternoon, if you take mine next Thursday. *Great*, I thought. *I'll clean and iron. . . .* My friend suggested that I "go smell a few roses."

I went to the park and stayed for a concert. But I felt a little guilty, and deep inside I worried a bit—were you all right?

I arrived back to find you busily playing with my friend's little girl. Now we're home, refreshed by our time apart. I need time for myself sometimes, Little One, but I praise God I have you to come home to.

> **H**e makes me
> lie down in
> green pastures,
> he leads me
> beside quiet waters.
>
> PSALM 23:2

## My Thoughts, Feelings, and Prayers for My Baby

.....................................................................

.....................................................................

.....................................................................

.....................................................................

.....................................................................

.....................................................................

.....................................................................

.....................................................................

.....................................................................

.....................................................................

.....................................................................

.....................................................................

.....................................................................

.....................................................................

.....................................................................

.....................................................................

.....................................................................

.....................................................................

## One Year Old Today!

*I* watch you in your crib, playing your early morning games, unaware that I am there. Then you look up, see me in the door. Instantly you pull yourself up, bounce up and down in joy, shrieking, "Mama! Mama! Mama!" What a marvelous way to start the day!

Is this what praise is all about? Is it just the natural way we humans react when we suddenly sense the presence of someone we adore? There are times when God seems so near that I want to jump up and down and stretch my arms toward him crying, "Lord! Lord! Lord!" Praise is love and adoration spontaneously pouring out of us, simply because our Beloved IS.

Does God need our praise? I don't know. But for all that he has been and will be, for all that he has taught me about himself this past year through you, my Child, I praise the Lord! PRAISE THE LORD!

> **Let everything that has breath praise the LORD. Praise the LORD.**
>
> PSALM 150:6